MW01490896

Summary and Analysis of

THE UNDERGROUND RAILROAD

Based on the Book
by Colson Whitehead

WORTH BOOKS
SMART SUMMARIES

This Worth Books book is based on the 2016 hardcover edition of *The Underground Railroad* by Colson Whitehead, published by Doubleday.

Summary and analysis copyright © 2017 by Open Road Integrated Media, Inc.

ISBN: 978-1-5040-4659-6

Worth Books
180 Maiden Lane
Suite 8A
New York, NY 10038
www.worthbooks.com

WORTH BOOKS
SMART SUMMARIES

Worth Books is a division of Open Road Integrated Media, Inc.

Contents

Context

Slavery, America's original sin, has long lurked in the background of American literature, a topic too painful for some to confront head on and too shameful for others to discuss. Since the publication of *Uncle Tom's Cabin* in 1852, few novelists have approached it, though Toni Morrison's *Beloved* and Edward P. Jones's *The Known World* are notable for their commercial success and the academic praise they received.

Colson Whitehead's *The Underground Railroad* was published amid a renewed interest in the history of slavery and, particularly, the clandestine network that gives the novel its name. Whitehead's book came one year after Eric Foner's *Gateway to Freedom: The Hidden History of the Underground Railroad*. Meanwhile, in 2016, WGN America televised *Underground*, a historical drama about a group of slaves who reach freedom via the Underground Railroad. Four months before Whitehead's novel was released, the United States Treasury announced that the image of Harriet Tubman—the most famous conductor of the historical Underground Railroad—would replace that of Andrew Jackson on the twenty-dollar bill.

The Underground Railroad won the 2016 National Book Award for fiction, appeared on many bestseller lists, and engaged readers in an original and timely slave narrative. Though it was written and published more than a century after the Civil War and the abolition of slavery, echoes of oppression, marginalization, and prejudice still abound in the current-day practices of stop-and-frisk, mass incarceration of people of color, and racial discrimination in and outside of the American criminal justice system.

Overview

The Underground Railroad breaks the uneasy silence about slavery with a realistic, shockingly brutal portrait of slave life, told as a historical fantasy.

Colson Whitehead has taken slavery's most famous metaphor and turned it into a reality. His underground railroad is a vast, physical rail system that transports runaways through miles of subterranean tunnels to different states of freedom. For the reader, boarding this train demands a suspension of disbelief; once made, it serves as transport to unexpected places, combining the brutal realities of slavery with a fabled version of history in a uniquely American version of magical realism.

Whitehead's heroine is Cora, a teenage slave whose mother, Mabel, vanished from the plantation that was their home, and their prison, in pre–Civil War Georgia. Cora hates her mother for abandoning her, but, emboldened by Mabel's success, she flees on the Underground Railroad. Her nemesis is Arnold Ridgeway, an infamous slave hunter who views his calling as a small contribution to something he calls "the American imperative." Cora's desperation and courage contrast with Ridgeway's offhanded cruelty as he pursues her across a landscape of historical events that have been retold to accommodate the narrative.

In South Carolina, the first stop on her journey, Cora encounters an apparently liberal slave regime that disguises a vast social experiment to control the black population, foreshadowing the eugenics programs that would take place a half century later. She escapes to North Carolina, where a less-subtle method of population control is employed in the form of weekly lynchings, served up as entertainment. Captured by Ridgeway, Cora is taken across the barren landscape of Tennessee, following the Trail of Tears traveled by the Cherokee nation.

Cora escapes Ridgeway and again rides the underground railway, this time to Indiana, where she first enjoys freedom on a communal farm populated by runaway slaves. Following an apocalyptic attack by white settlers and a violent confrontation with Ridgeway, she heads west to California, leaving the reader wondering what degree of freedom she will finally attain—and whether the slave catcher will continue to pursue her.

The success of *The Underground Railroad* lies not only in its original take on history, but also in its descriptions of the internal worlds of the slaves themselves. Their lives are an endless routine of monotonous labor broken by incidents of unspeakable cruelty, "travesties so routine and familiar that they were a kind of weather." However, their ability to turn hopelessness into courage is what makes *The Underground Railroad* such a compelling story, a fantastical journey laden with uncomfortable truths.

Cast of Characters

Ajarry: Cora's grandmother who was kidnapped in Africa and taken on a slave ship to the United States, where she was sold several times before entering the Randall plantation.

Aloysius Stevens: A doctor from Boston who tends to Cora while she is in South Carolina and suggests that she consider being sterilized. Later, we learn that he is part of a vast movement to control the slave population.

Arnold Ridgeway: The slave catcher tasked by the Randalls with recapturing Cora's mother, Mabel—a mission at which he fails. Cora's escape provides him with a chance to redeem himself.

Caesar: An educated slave from Virginia who was "sold down the river" to Georgia; he proposes that Cora and he flee the Randall plantation together.

Cora: The protagonist; a female slave on the Randall plantation. Her mother, Mabel, has vanished, filling Cora with resentment for being abandoned, but also with the hope that she can escape, too.

John Valentine: The mixed-race owner of a communal farm for runaways in Indiana, where Cora enjoys freedom for the first time.

Lovey: Cora's friend on the Randall plantation; when Cora and Caesar escape, Lovey follows, but she is captured when the three are attacked by bounty hunters.

Martin Wells: The underground railroad's station agent in North Carolina. He and his wife, Ethel, hide Cora in the attic of their home until all three are later discovered.

Royal: A freeman who works for the underground railroad; he rescues Cora from Ridgeway in Tennessee and delivers her to freedom in Indiana, where he begins to court her.

Sam: A white bartender and agent of the underground railroad; he aids Cora and Caesar when they arrive in South Carolina.

Terrance Randall: The younger of the two Randall brothers; dissolute and given to acts of wanton cruelty, Terrance becomes sole owner of the plantation after his brother James's death.

Summary

Ajarry

Caesar, a slave on the Randall plantation in Georgia, suggests that Cora and he flee together to the North. Her refusal prompts a flashback to the story of her grandmother Ajarry, who was kidnapped in her native Benin and taken onboard a slave ship to South Carolina.

During the course of her lifetime, Ajarry was bought and sold many times. She came to understand that slaves were literally objects: Their value was determined by their usefulness. Ajarry's own value as a woman, she reasoned, was that she could bring more slaves into the world; however, all of her children died, with the exception of Cora's mother, Mabel.

Georgia

Cora's mother disappears when she is eleven years old, leaving the girl adrift in plantation slave life. The only link she has to her family is a tiny garden plot that was tended by both her mother and grandmother.

When a young slave places a doghouse on the site, Cora destroys it with a hatchet and then confronts the slave. The incident earns Cora a reputation as a madwoman, someone not to be trifled with.

When Terrance Randall, one of the plantation's owners, beats a slave boy with a cane, Cora throws her body over the child to take the punishment herself. This merits her a blow to the face from Terrance's cane—and whippings on the days that follow.

Here we learn that Mabel, Cora's mother, was not sold, but escaped from the Randall plantation. To sustain herself during her journey, Mabel dug up every sweet potato from her vegetable garden. For Cora, the tiny patch of land became not only a source of sustenance, but also a source of hope that she might one day be reunited with her mother.

When Cora realizes that Terrance Randall has decided to take her for a mistress, she accepts Caesar's proposal to flee. The following night, they depart the plantation. Lovey, Cora's friend, secretly follows the pair through the swamp.

The next night, the three are surprised by a group of bounty hunters. Cora kills one, and she and Caesar manage to escape, but Lovey is captured. Cora and Caesar make it to the house of a white man, Fletcher, who takes them to the next stop on their journey: a barn with a secret tunnel that leads to an improbable destination—a railroad, buried deep under the ground, that will transport them to freedom.

Ridgeway

Arnold Ridgeway, a blacksmith's son, found his calling as a teenager when he joined the "patrollers," who scoured the back roads of Georgia, hunting down runaway slaves. Ridgeway quickly graduated from patroller to slave hunter, traveling north to retrieve runaways from the free states and return them to their owners for rewards. His skill at tracking down slaves and his legendary cruelty earn him mythical status among slaves.

Ridgeway has formed his own gang of slave catchers who, in spite of interference from abolitionists and courts in the North, rarely failed to recapture an escapee. One of the few exceptions was Cora's mother, Mabel, whose freedom Ridgeway regards as a personal failure. Cora's escape convinces Ridgeway that the underground railroad must be operating in Georgia.

South Carolina

Cora and Caesar arrive by locomotive in South Carolina, a state with liberal views regarding "colored advancement." Aided by Sam, a white man who is a member of the underground railroad, the pair assumes new identities, finds jobs, and lives essentially as free people, although in segregation.

They receive free medical treatment, during which the men are submitted to frequent blood tests and the women are encouraged to consider sterilization. Later, Sam discovers that the former slaves are guinea pigs in a vast experiment to control the size of black population (which, by 1810, was nearly equal to the white population in South Carolina).

Shortly after, Ridgeway arrives in town, and Cora escapes capture by descending again into the tunnel that leads to the underground railroad, but Caesar is left behind.

Stevens

Dr. Aloysius Stevens, the physician who Cora met with in South Carolina, paid for his medical studies with a part-time job as a body snatcher's assistant. He helps

Carpenter, a rough-hewn Irishman, to rob gravesites to supply cadavers to medical schools, where they are used for dissection and anatomy classes.

Body snatching was a lucrative business, and the corpses of colored men and women were the easiest prey, as their families would not resort to the law to reclaim them. However, Stevens realizes that only in death are the black man and the white man equal. When a student inserts his scapula into the cadaver of a black man, it's then, in death, that the corpse becomes a human being.

North Carolina

Cora's next stop is North Carolina, where she hides in the attic of a house owned by another white abolitionist, Martin Wells. Through a peephole, she witnesses a horrifying spectacle: the lynching of a runaway slave girl in the presence of cheering white townspeople. Cora soon discovers that this is a regular event called the Friday Festival. Martin explains that North Carolina is bent on eliminating the black population and having their work done by Irish or German immigrants.

Cora's time in the attic reminds readers of *The Diary of Anne Frank*, in which the Frank family is protected from capture by a few thin walls and the kindness of strangers. However, Cora's confinement ends when Fiona, an Irish maid who works in the Wellses' house, tells the night riders that she suspects Martin and his wife, Ethel, are harboring a runaway.

The night riders, who have already searched the Wellses' house once, return as the Friday Festival is taking place. The Wells are tied to a tree, and Cora is taken away by a posse of slave catchers, led by Ridgeway, who are intent on returning her to the Randall plantation in Georgia.

Ethel

This brief chapter contains a character study of Ethel, Martin Wells's wife. Her marriage to Martin was troubled by his decision to carry on his father's work helping runaways to escape to freedom, something she disapproved of. She grew up in a slave-owning family, but harbored a childhood fantasy about becoming a missionary in Africa. However, Africa comes to her in the body of Cora, whom she helps nurse back to health, in spite of her misgivings about aiding runaway slaves.

Tennessee

Ridgeway and his band of slave catchers—a freed boy, Homer, and a white slave hunter, Boseman—begin the long journey to take Cora and another recaptured slave, Jasper, to their masters. However, instead of going south, they head west through Tennessee, along the Trail of Tears and Death traveled by the Cherokee nation on its forced march to Oklahoma.

From Ridgeway, Cora learns that Lovey, the girl who had escaped with her from the plantation, was recaptured and executed by Terrance Randall. Ridgeway despises Randall for his gratuitous violence, but he shocks Cora when he murders the other runaway, Jasper, before her eyes.

The band of travelers arrives at a small town, and Ridgeway takes Cora to supper in a tavern, expounding his philosophies on life and justifying his grim trade. On the way out of town, the slave-hunting party is attacked by Royal, a freeman, and two runaways. Ridgeway is left in chains and Cora flees with the attackers.

Caesar

This brief chapter, written from Caesar's point of view in the past, describes his love for Cora. He was attracted by her beauty and, being a woodworker, dreamed of carving a sculpture of her. Caesar also admired Cora's courage, which he saw firsthand when she tried to protect the slave boy from Randall's blows. Caesar, who had once enjoyed a status near to that of a freeman, knew that Cora's courage and determination would be essential to his own escape.

Indiana

The action jumps forward in time and place to Indiana, where Cora is living on a large communal farm owned by a family of freemen, the Valentines. Cora continues to inquire about her mother among the other runaways, but she finds no answers. She works at various tasks, including childcare, farming, and doing laundry. She also pursues her education, but her future remains uncertain.

Royal, the freeman who rescued Cora from Ridgeway, courts her. He takes Cora to the terminus of the underground railroad, prompting a recollection of her escape. She tells him she doesn't want to run anymore and that she's content on the Valentine farm, but Royal intimates that now that she has been saved by the underground railroad, she must become a part of it.

Sam, the white man who had helped Cora escape South Carolina, appears at the farm and gives her some welcomed news: Terrance Randall is dead. Ridgeway, the infamous slave hunter, is still alive, but he lives in disgrace because of Cora's escape in Tennessee.

But Ridgeway soon reappears, this time among a group of white men who attack the Valentine farm, murdering many of the residents and scaring off the rest. Cora is recaptured by the slave hunter.

Mabel

In another flashback chapter, we discover what Cora will never know—that her mother, Mabel, died in the swamp bordering the Randall plantation on the night of her escape. Mabel felt freedom for a few brief moments, but she was tortured by the fact that she had left her daughter behind. She turned back, hoping to reach the plantation before she was missed. Instead, Mabel was bitten by a poisonous snake, and her body slid into a bed of moss, where it would remain undiscovered.

The North

As the carnage at the Valentine farm continues, Ridgeway forces Cora to show him to the entry to the underground railroad. On the steps down to the platform, Cora struggles with Ridgeway, and they both fall to the bottom. Ridgeway sustains a severe head injury, allowing Cora to escape by using the handcar parked on the nearby rails.

After pumping for hours, an exhausted Cora finds a way out of the tunnel. Upon emerging, she encounters a family of white settlers traveling west to California. A black man driving one of their wagons invites her to come aboard. The novel closes as Cora begins yet another stage in her long journey to freedom.

Character Analysis

Caesar: *The Underground Railroad*'s most sympathetic and tragic character, Caesar is an educated slave who had hoped to be freed in his native Virginia, but was instead sold to the Randall plantation in Georgia. The chapter on Caesar reveals both his love for Cora and his admiration for her courage, telling as much about her as it does about him.

Cora: The book's protagonist, Cora is a courageous heroine tortured by a past of abandonment and abuse. Her determination to reach freedom leads her to commit acts of bravery that might otherwise be characterized as reckless. In Georgia, she takes a beating meant for a slave boy, only to suffer a brutal whipping herself afterward. Cora achieves freedom thanks to Royal, a brave man who courts her, but she is unable to return his love because of her deep-seated distrust of men.

Terrance Randall: A villain out of central casting, Terrance is a pathologically violent, shamelessly lustful slave owner, complete with a white linen suit and silver-tipped cane. His cruelty, and the knowledge that he wants Cora as his mistress, ultimately convinces Cora that she must escape from his plantation.

Arnold Ridgeway: At six feet six, Ridgeway is a physically dominant, larger-than-life villain who inhabits the story. Even in his absence, he stands for all that is foul about the system of slavery in America. His failure to capture Mabel, Cora's mother, haunts him like a curse, and capturing Cora is the only way he can break it. Ridgeway is a complex character with a set of cynical rationalizations to justify his work. He is also resilient; he's capable of recovering from both defeat and disgrace.

Sam: A jovial South Carolina bartender, Sam risks his life to help Cora and Caesar during their stay in his state. He later reappears in Indiana, where he tells Cora that Caesar was killed and that Terrance Randall, her former owner, has also died. Sam's role serves to answer questions that have been left open about other characters.

Themes and Symbols

Themes

Loss and love: Slavery deprived Cora of much more than her freedom, her past, and her mother; it also rendered her unable to love. The experience of being raped by plantation slaves when she was a teenager gives her an inherent distrust and fear of men. This makes her incapable of returning the affections of the decent men she encounters on her journey: Caesar, who convinces her to flee, and Royal, who rescues her from Ridgeway.

Silence: Slavery was an enormously cruel and unjust institution, but it was not a crime; on the contrary, it was the law of the land, which most people obeyed, if not unquestioningly. The white abolitionists who help Cora on the road to freedom are conflicted (some even come from slave-owning families) but prepared to face the consequences of their actions. Their moral courage contains a silent indictment of those who didn't participate in slavery but enjoyed its economic benefits nonetheless.

Symbols

The land: Cora's only physical connection to her past and her family is a three-square-yard garden plot that was tended by her mother and her grandmother. The "field" provides a bit of extra sustenance in the form of yams and okra, which both Mabel and Cora took along on their respective flights to freedom. One might also consider the land that Dr. Stevens and others used to harvest the bodies of black men and women for their medical research.

The railroad: The literal underground railroad was a project that required enormous physical labor of the kind that slaves were required to provide daily on Southern plantations. When Cora first sees the railroad, she contrasts it with the slaves' work in the cotton harvest: "It was a magnificent operation, from seed to bale, but not one of them could be prideful of their labor. It had been stolen from them. Bled from them." Whitehead is careful not to overwhelm the story with the railroad; instead, he uses it sparingly, casting it as symbol of courage and bravery.

The printed word: In South Carolina, Cora learns to read, and she continues to practice when she reaches Indiana. Although reading opens a world of knowledge to her, she is also struck by the falsehoods on the printed page, including those contained in the Declaration of Independence: "We hold these truths to be self-evident, that all men are created equal . . ."

Author's Style

Whitehead begins the novel in a concise, third-person narrative style peppered with allusions to historical events and places (Ouidah, Sullivan's Island, Dahomey). As the story progresses, he grows more lyrical, as in Cora's recollection of the cotton harvest in Georgia: "The vast fields burst with hundreds of thousands of white bolls, strung like stars in the sky on the clearest of clear nights. When the slaves finished, they had stripped the fields of their color."

The chapters are of varying length, with the longest ones devoted to the places Cora stops on her quest for freedom: Georgia, South Carolina, North Carolina, Tennessee, and Indiana. Each state in the story presents a slightly different attitude toward slaves, exposing Cora to a broad spectrum of experiences—some much more brutal than others. Interspersed are short chapters that combine profiles of the characters with flashbacks. These changes in point of view and time disrupt the narrative, adding tension to an already suspenseful story.

The main element of magical realism in *The Underground Railroad* is the author's presentation of the network of people and places that protected slaves and helped them journey northward to freedom, which has been transformed into an actual subterranean transportation system. This is balanced with historical details, including reproductions of actual advertisements offering reward money for the return of runaway slaves.

Direct Quotes and Analysis

"*Sometimes a slave will be lost in a brief eddy of liberation. In the sway of a sudden reverie among the furrows or while untangling the mysteries of an early-morning dream. In the middle of a song on a warm Sunday night. Then it comes, always—the overseer's cry, the call to work, the shadow of the master.*"

Cora reflects on the brief moments of respite in the life of a slave. Slavery ensures that her life does not belong to her, that she is at the beck and call of her master. Yet, here, she is presented as a human being in nature, appreciative of the world around her. Passages like this one, in which Whitehead describes the emotional and psychological world of the slaves, are among the most memorable in the novel.

"He maintained a serene comportment at all times but generated a threatening atmosphere, like a thunderhead that seems far away but then is suddenly overhead with loud violence."

This is Whitehead's first description of Ridgeway, the slave catcher whose presence looms over the novel. Like Herman Melville's Captain Ahab in *Moby-Dick* or the film *Apocalypse Now*'s Colonel Kurtz, Ridgeway is an enigmatic villain, apparently rational yet gripped by an obsession that prompts frequent and unexpected explosions of violence. The invocation of the thunderhead, a force of nature, is also apt in that its malevolence is always in motion, and the sight of one portends that a storm is on its way.

"Fletcher had undertaken a great risk for them, even when the situation grew more complicated than he had bargained. The only currency to satisfy the debt was their survival and to help others when circumstances permitted."

Cora describes the feeling of responsibility—more than gratitude—that she and Caesar feel toward Fletcher, the white abolitionist who brought them to the underground railroad. The risks he took to help them could only be made worthwhile if they finally achieved their freedom, and if they, in turn, offered the same compassion and protection to others.

"The underground railroad maintained no lines to speak of. The decoys in negro dress, the secret codes in the back pages of the newspapers. They openly bragged of their subversion, hustling a slave out the back door as the slave catchers broke down the front. It was a criminal conspiracy devoted to theft of property, and Ridgeway suffered their brazenness as a personal slur."

Ridgeway's view of the underground railroad reflects not just popular sentiment, but also the prevailing law. The runaways and the abolitionists who aided them were technically criminals. Ridgeway's occupation, on the other hand, was a legal one, justified by the Fugitive Slave Act of 1850, which ruled that slaves who escaped to free states remained the property of their masters.

"Running away was a transgression so large that the punishment enveloped every generous soul on her brief tour of freedom."

Cora, after being recaptured by Ridgeway, thinks about the misfortunes that befell all the people who tried to help her to freedom. Caesar was killed by a mob and the Wellses were stoned to death outside their home. All the virtuous and courageous individuals she encountered suffered terribly for helping her.

Trivia

1. Sullivan's Island, where Cora's grandmother Ajarry entered the United States, was known as the "Ellis Island of slavery." It was the entry point for some 40% of the four hundred thousand African slaves who entered the United States from 1619 until the importation of slaves ended in 1808.

2. The number of African slaves brought to the United States pales in comparison to the four million slaves who were imported to Brazil, which, in 1888, became the last country in the West to abolish slavery.

3. In the chapter titled Tennessee, Cora and Ridge-way travel along the Trail of Tears and Death, the route followed by the Cherokee tribe on a forced march to Oklahoma in 1838. The Cherokee also kept African American slaves, some of whom made this tragic journey. By the 1860s, some eight thousand black slaves lived on Indian territories, comprising 14% of the population.

4. Harriet Tubman, the real-life "conductor" of the Underground Railroad, not only helped hundreds of slaves to freedom, she also served in the Union Army as a cook, nurse, and scout during the Civil War. In June 1863, Tubman guided Union troops into combat during a successful raid on Comba-hee Ferry, South Carolina, in which seven hun-dred and fifty slaves were freed.

5. In an August 2016 interview, author Colson Whitehead recognized the debt he owes to the magical realism of Latin American novelists. Before writing *The Underground Railroad*, he reread Gabriel García Marquez's *One Hundred Years of Solitude*.

6. Colson Whitehead said that becoming a father was one of the reasons he finally wrote *The Under-ground Railroad*, a novel he had thought about for fifteen years. Fatherhood forced him to imagine what slavery might be like—the terrible pain of separation from a parent or a child, or the pain of seeing a loved one brutalized.

7. During colonial times, before slaves could escape to freedom in the northern states, many fled from plantations and formed communities that survived for decades, despite repeated attempts to destroy them. About fifty such "maroon societies" existed in the South between 1672 and the end of the Civil War. One of the largest was located in the Great Dismal Swamp, a two-hundred-square-mile area between North Carolina and Virginia that provided refuge to thousands of escaped slaves until it was finally drained in the 1780s and 1790s.

8. The US National Park Service has established a nationwide Network to Freedom program that brings together historical sites, museums, and other facilities associated with the Underground Railroad. As of September 2014, the network included three hundred and eighty historic sites located in thirty-six states and Washington, DC. The National Underground Railroad Freedom Center, the first museum devoted exclusively to the topic, was inaugurated in Cincinnati in 2004.

9. Perhaps the most extraordinary escape on the Underground Railroad was made by Henry "Box" Brown, a slave from Richmond, Virginia. Brown had a friend, Samuel Smith, nail him into a three-foot-long wooden box and ship it to the Vigilance Committee, an abolitionist group in Philadelphia. After a twenty-seven-hour trip inside the box—labeled "This Side Up with Care"—Brown arrived at his destination and became a free man.

10. Although the Underground Railroad ran south to north, many African Americans escaped slavery by heading south to Florida. A Spanish colony until 1821, Florida offered runaway slaves freedom provided they pledged allegiance to the King of Spain and converted to Catholicism.

What's That Word?

Ashanti: An ethnic group native to the Ashanti region of modern-day Ghana. Mary, a slave who cared for Cora after she was whipped on the Randall plantation, was descended from Ashanti stock, as were her two husbands.

Coffle: A group of animals or slaves tied together. After being sold to a slave trader in Charleston, Cora's grandmother Ajarry was marched to her next destination in a coffle behind the trader's cart.

Cowrie shells: Brightly colored, polished seashells used as jewelry or money in certain parts of Africa. After she was captured in her native village, Ajarry was traded in exchange for cowrie shells several times before being sold to the European slavers at the port of Ouidah in Benin.

Dahomey: A West African kingdom that existed from 1600 to 1894. Raiders from Dahomey entered Ajarry's village and took her and the other inhabitants off to be sold as slaves.

Gold Coast: An area of the west coast of Africa that corresponds roughly to present-day Ghana. The majority of the African slaves who arrived in North America, including Ajarry, came directly from this area.

Goofer: To cast a spell on someone or something; to hex; or to use "goofer dust" to carry out such a spell. When Cora's mother, Mabel, escapes from the Randall plantation, Terrance Randall hires a witch to goofer the boundaries of the property so that no one with African blood can leave without being stricken by palsy.

Ouidah: A city on the Atlantic coast of modern-day Benin, from which Ajarry, Cora's grandmother, departs for America on a slave ship. A former Portuguese colonial outpost, Ouidah was a major center of the slave trade.

Sullivan's Island: An island off the coast of South Carolina, near Charleston Bay; it was the largest entry point for African slaves brought to North America. Ajarry spent a month in the "pest house" on Sullivan's Island. Once certified as being clear of contagion, she was sold at an auction in Charleston.

Critical Response

- Winner of the Pulitzer Prize for Fiction
- Winner of the National Book Award for Fiction
- #1 *New York Times* bestseller
- Oprah's Book Club 2016 selection

"I haven't been as simultaneously moved and entertained by a book for many years. This is a luminous, furious, wildly inventive tale that not only shines a bright light on one of the darkest periods of history, but also opens up thrilling new vistas for the form of the novel itself." —*The Guardian*

"[Whitehead] has told a story essential to our understanding of the American past and the American present." —*The New York Times*

"*The Underground Railroad* reanimates the slave narrative, disrupts our settled sense of the past and stretches the ligaments of history right into our own era."

—*The Washington Post*

"*The Underground Railroad* perfectly balances the realism of its subject with fabulist touches that render it freshly illuminating. Whitehead's rails carry Cora not just from state to state but also through time, opening multiple chapters of black life in America."

—*Time*

"Whitehead continues the African-American artists' inquiry into race mythology and history with rousing audacity and razor-sharp ingenuity; he is now assuredly a writer of the first rank."   —*Kirkus Reviews*

"Lovely and rare, dark and imaginative, *The Underground Railroad* is Whitehead's best work and an important American novel."   —*The Boston Globe*

"In imagining how things might have been in an alternate historical reality, Whitehead reminds us of the horrors, hopes, and leaps of faith that shaped the actual experiences of early African Americans—and which reverberate to this day."   —*The Seattle Times*

About Colson Whitehead

Born in 1969, Colson Whitehead grew up in Manhattan. After attending Harvard College, he started writing for the *Village Voice* in New York City. While working as a journalist, he began writing novels, the first of which, *The Intuitionist,* was published in 1999 to widespread critical acclaim—including from John Updike, who called Whitehead "the young African American writer to watch."

The Intuitionist was followed the novel *John Henry Days,* a Pulitzer Prize finalist; *The Colossus of New York,* a book of essays; *Apex Hides the Hurt*; *Sag Harbor*; and *Zone One.* In 2014, Whitehead published a nonfiction account of the world series of poker, *The Noble Hustle: Poker, Beef Jerky, and Death.*

Whitehead has taught at a number of universities, among them Princeton, New York University, Columbia, and Wesleyan, and he was a Writer-in-Residence at Vassar College. He has also been the recipient of numerous awards, including the Whiting Award, a MacArthur Fellowship, the John Dos Passos Prize, and a Guggenheim Fellowship.

For Your Information

Online

"10 Unapologetic Books About Race in America." EarlyBirdBooks.com

"Colson Whitehead on Slavery, Success and Writing the Novel That Scared Him." NYTimes.com

"Colson Whitehead's 'Underground Railroad' Is a Literal Train to Freedom." NPR.org

"Colson Whitehead on His Spectacular New Novel, *The Underground Railroad*." Vogue.com

"In Conversation with Colson Whitehead." Vulture.com

"The Perilous Lure of the Underground Railroad." TheNewYorker.com

"The Secret History of the Underground Railroad." TheAtlantic.com

"Underground Railroad." History.com

Books

Beloved by Toni Morrison

Bound for the Promised Land: Harriet Tubman: Portrait of an American Hero by Katherine Clifford Larson

Confessions of Nat Turner by William Styron

The Color Purple by Alice Walker

Gateway to Freedom: The Hidden History of the Underground Railroad by Eric Foner

The Known World by Edward P. Jones

Twelve Years a Slave by Solomon Northup

The Underground Railroad: Authentic Narratives and First-Hand Accounts by William Still

Bibliography

Goodheart, Adam. "The Secret History of the Under-
    ground Railroad." *The Atlantic Monthly*. March
    2015. Accessed December 20, 2015. http://www
    .theatlantic.com/magazine/archive/2015/03
    /the-secret-history-of-the-underground-railroad
    /384966/.
Lockley, Tim. "Runaway Slave Communities in South
    Carolina." History in Focus. Accessed December
    21, 2016. https://www.history.ac.uk/ihr/Focus
    /Slavery/articles/lockley.html.
National Parks Service Network to Freedom website.
    Accessed December 20, 2016. https://www.nps
    .gov/subjects/ugrr/index.htm.

National Underground Railroad Freedom Center website. Accessed December 21, 2016. http://freedomcenter.org.

Schulz, Kathryn. "The Perilous Lure of the Underground Railroad." *The New Yorker*, August 22, 2016. Accessed December 21, 2016. http://www.newyorker.com/magazine/2016/08/22/the-perilous-lure-of-the-underground-railroad.

WORTH BOOKS

SMART SUMMARIES

So much to read,
so little time?

Explore summaries of bestselling
fiction and essential nonfiction
books on a variety of subjects,
including business, history, science,
lifestyle, and much more.

Visit the store at
www.ebookstore.worthbooks.com

MORE SMART SUMMARIES
FROM WORTH BOOKS

CONTEMPORARY FICTION

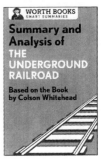

WORTH BOOKS
SMART SUMMARIES

CPSIA information can be obtained
at www.ICGtesting.com
Printed in the USA
LVOW07s2131120917
548366LV00034B/66/P

9 781504 046596